Poetry Journey Experience

Creative poems

Luwonda Dews-Benninger

BookLeaf Publishing

India | USA | UK

Made with ❤ on the BookLeaf Publishing Platform
www.bookleafpub.in
www.bookleafpub.com

Dedication

I would like to thank some of the famous poets who I read and learned to write poetry from. They inspired me to write this book and other books.

Preface

If you are a poetry lover you will appreciate this book in your collection of unique reading pastime. The expression and rhythm will give you a pleasurable poetry experience. And you will feel the incredible poetic encounter because of how creative and imaginative the art of rhyme was well done. So fascinating that you will read it again and again as a enjoyable reading journey.

Acknowledgements

I want to acknowledge who first help me make my dreams come true by helping me get into the publishing industry. After having some disappointments and problems I found myself writing some series of poems. I never gave up on my passion for poetry as I went through a poetry journey experience. I continued to write unwavering with determination. One fateful night I happened to find my exquisite glitch and pleasurable extraordinary skillful.

1. The Beauty of the Glen

A good day feeling spirited seeing the scenery.
The blessed atmosphere of the peaceful pasture.
Shepherds faithful winsome guiding the way for sure.
To new pleasing fond foliage carefree and must-see.
Through predators, dangers and difficulties that occur.

Even with struggles again the beauty of the glen.
The sun shines divine as the flowers splendor shows.
The light on the graphite white river fancy flows.
A blessing as the grass grows and reflect in rows, when
As the whisk of the waterfront builds up and glows.
Thankful to God for grazing and what they found fine.
The fervent flowers in the thicket have height.
The colors cover the gorgeous glen site.
Flattering flowers truly newly align.
Not afraid, attractive and tasteful invite.
Trusting God the shepherds knowing to endure.
Sheep encouraged to follow through mountain and tree
Inspirited even through valley larger expansive agree.
Praising God back to the corral and secure.

After all the testing resting would be.

A good day feeling spirited seeing the scenery.
The blessed atmosphere of the peaceful pasture.
Shepherds faithfully winsomely guiding the way for
sure.
To new pleasing fond foliage carefree and must-see.
Through predators, dangers and difficulties that occur.
Even with struggles again the beauty of the glen.
The sun shines divine as the flowers splendor shows.
The light on the graphite white river fancy flows.
A blessing as the firm grass grows and reflect in rows,
when
As the whisk of the waterfront builds up and glows.
Thankful to God for grazing and what they found fine.
The fervent flowers in the thicket have height.
The colors cover the gorgeous glen site.
Flattering flowers truly newly align.
Not afraid, attractive and tasteful invite.
Trusting God the shepherds knowing to endure.
The sheep encouraged to follow through mountain and
tree
Inspirited even through valley larger expansive agree.
Praising God back to the <u>corral</u> and secure.
After all the testing resting would be.

2. Nature Walk Ballad

As I see an artwork of the summer sunrise
Across the heartened spellbound horizon
To the gleams and beams of the dazzling distant sun
A feeling of fascinating perky peace was a surprise.
New day motivated to go on a walk as the sun redone.
You can hear the sound of the river whispering in the
sunlight.
With the sunlight bright and the beauty of the brook
blend
Pleasing misty music as Erato to take a friend.
Healthy spite air on the spectacular site.
Amble ramble adventure around the river bend.
Awakening to the uplifted mountainous range
breathtaking
Maintained unplain fruit forest to gallivant.
Blissful leaves in the breeze beautiful chime and chant.
Pretty plenteous mountain plane peacemaking.
As if it gained an effect of a gallery to enchant.

3. Winsomeness of the Woods

In the winsomeness of the woods upon awakening
I saw the leaves decorative dancing in a stir.
Flashy expensive, they skipped around her
Circled her many times in merry making
Played the instrument, sang a song and adjure.
O hear the gorgeous sound gather near the trees.
Escape into the soft sound about
The forest whisk of the wind fade-out
To the feeling of lively fine flowers in sceneries
As if I can touch a fancy flower that stands-out.

4. Garden Impression

Garden pond flowing with flowers all around.
A blanket of flowers near with the sun's ray.
A bright bird in the garden with a serene sound.
A delightful mist was on the flowers today.
Enchanting flourishing flowers cascade the yard.
A quiet flowing rock garden sparkles' with sun.
Then seen mirror-like the fish splash in slightly hard.
Observe occasional flower floating upon.
New peaceful midsummer flowers retreat.
Naturally flowing pond so softly heard.
Darling garden fountain, oh how so sweet.
And lifted my spirit to hear a songbird
Joyful light smell of flowers never end
Pleasurable inner calm beyond question
Growing flowers in an exceptional blend
Which forms as a good lyrical reflection.
Warm welcome around the flowers as they grow.
So pleasant as if a musical garden.
With a natural beauty, the tranquil flow.
Then a couple went out on a date again.

The lady went to the restaurant from a child.
Then, ordered some food that manifests the best.
And saw a vase of flowers sweet, neat and mild.
She said, "You have lovelier flowers, I'm impressed."
Enjoying the delicious food was true.
With its exclusive high ceilings and light.
She was very fashionable everyday.
She said, "I like the flowers throughout, they are new".
He said, "They are from your garden, are they alright"?
They laughed; she said surprised, "they made my day"

5. Love Letter in the Garden Sonnet

Her beloved wrote her a letter.
She walked to the bright garden to read it.
And grabbed a light costly crocheted sweater.
Full of fresh air, flowers windblown and sunlit.
She looked at the pendant matching her outfit.
Pleasing manner, quiet, and love stirred.
Found near the beautiful blooms a place to sit.
Delightful as music a passing songbird.
Lovely feeling freedom harkened and heard
She took off her sweater, it was a warm day.
A nice pattern with a hint of textured.
Passionately waiting to hear what he had to say.
A big budding tree was used for shade
Tall and resonant its shadow became
Actively, a lyric pastime was made
As the pansies and petunias reclaim
As if the garden was a meadow the same
Walking through the growth of grass with care;
As the hurried hummingbird's song acclaim;

With frequent fragrant flowers in the air
A tasteful scarf around the waist to wear
Shifting possessing a small floral style;
Drawn to a river with a touch of glare.
Reflecting upon our youth in the meanwhile
Near a floral hill the small garden seating.
Held the letter dreaming of hearsay;
Opening the letter with its greeting.
He told her, he would meet her soon someday.
My strong endless love will make away.
His love was infinite he had to admit.
I am not halfway; I will meet you shipway.
I miss you as the waves flow tideway moonlit.
And love you forever shining as starlit.
And my love I will on and on proclaim.
He wanted to marry her as it befit.
Love fully ignites as a burning flame
She looked up from the letter, she heard a voice.
Happy to hear her love standing near, she rejoiced.

6. Dance and Sing

Dance all night; try it if you wished or dared.
to the mellow music couples danced paired.
Actress came into the camera to perform.
Notably she danced with chic rhythm form.
Good and genuine energy she possess.
Challenge, danced around the area with progress
all of a sudden, noticing moves she made
she was asked to sing for the crowd urged to persuade
The gal sang with merriment all nightlong
she said pertly, "how do you like the song"?
Girl persuaded the people to sing and chant
Nice the music was chosen to enchant.
Repeating her they sounded well as she wished.
Joined in with the prima-donna rolled offish.
Lovely girl helped them since they opened the curtain.
Needing her help to sing all night was certain.
Sounding beautiful drawn to the music, therefore.
With excitement you could see an open door.
Singing a new song in came a man clean.
He started to sing with a dancing routine.

Hands clapping he sound good, strong and came near.
The crowd liked what they heard; they sound sincere.
Singing magnetize the music, they disappeared.
Then the door opened; they both reappeared.
And they came in with many dancers quick.
Singing as a whole group with a dancing trick.
Still in turn and in unison shifting.
Enjoyed a lively act with the night drifting.

7. Beautiful Hills Ode

I love the hills they are broad and breathtaking.
It's a beautiful day as they ramble long.
Meanwhile the hills and valleys peacemaking.
Its' magnitude is great as a stunning song.
The trees near the hills and the flowers.
With the beautiful hills with the sunrise.
And it certainly possessed peace for hours.
And as pleasing music found to arise.
The pretty trees in the meadows surround
As a musical display of cadence
Water down a slope before the night bound.
Feeling of fantasy the hills distance.
Lovely smell of the hills after the rain.
As healthy washing as Paeon flabbergast.
The grass, trees and flowers mix and explain.
Like a painting of the hills so colorfast.
Wondering through and grasping the high view.
Looking and exploring everywhere.
Watching the slopes and waiting for you.
As my heart lifts new with life's care.

astonishing day as our love became.
You are as my desire for broad hills and field.
Personal journey to see nature obtain.
Enjoy each other's company the same.
Scenery to socialize, laugh and be healed.
Dream of meeting you and memories remain.

8. Love of Nature Sonnet

O, nature has love and sweet happiness;
Finding the warm love around here.
Thus, so pleasant and I profess;
As the pretty flower buds grow so near;
As a soft sound of the stream we hear.
And impressed and amply address.
The flowers in the forest had no compare.
They were as lovely as a babbling brook.
See it sparkle at night as the stars look.
The smell of a garden after the rain.
Gentle genteel garden as a hidden hook.
The colors of the flowers love can explain.
Feelings as I favor you, I can express.
And the thoughts of things beautiful I guess.

9. I Have Seen them In the Summer

I looked out the window at the placid sky.
And heard the windblown trees sound as a bell;
As the moors swayed in the wind nearby;
The maple and berry-like trees in the dell.
A high cloud veiled the sun above a mount.
Life in the spacious summer takes effect.
As the color stands on the hills surmount.
Shows many mystical mountain's respect.
Bemuse deep depth in the valley dwell.
The woods crooked creek sounds remain
Near the intensity of nature's well
The new tones of the trees after the rain.
And a distinct bud on a branch exists.
A flounced flower peaked through the growth ground
Two-toned trees gleam near a stream with a twist
Suddenly peace as an Edda song around.
Rejoicing in substance of life's charade.
Conveying a mild musical feeling near.
wind shifting with the coarse the river made.

Flowers and rocks edging the river here.
As I often think of you; as you knew.
Desirously drawn to you, day and night.
Oh, yes my livened love is simply true.
Thus my feelings are so infinite.
As the many stars my love will always grow.
Fascinated by you and the moon in space.
As the continual celestial glow.
I see your love forever in this place.
I thought about you and the countryside view.
admired and discovered you from afar.
and I hope you think about me too.
A relished burning and yearning so far.
My love for you, in the summer is great.
you are special to me; my heart did melt.
As a flower always blooms is our fate.
Morning to the dusk of day a mood is felt.
Your beauty as a wondering thought all-day.
Until it securely stays on my mind.
As a sprouting and blossoming bouquet.
Your unique inviting voice I find.
As Euterpe lovely music in rhyme
My love for you is a blissful jewel gift.
Waiting and longing to be with you sometime
My heart melts for your sweet miracle lift.
And I see your love forever growing.
In the long moments patiently waiting for you

The precious times with knack of knowing
And so that one day I will say I do.
I am fond of the type of friendly times spent
It is as if we will write a love ode.
I admire your emotional content.
Deciding to travel joint episode.
As an impressive couple going hence.
Lady in pink and the man sharp enthused.
Eager for an exciting weekend thence
Going on a generous trip amused.
To see a snug cottage on a summer day.
And claim the truly best room with care.
Hurrying past the sweet flowers on the way.
Remembering the inspiring house there.
The wind blows the musical leaves in the yard.
As the sun weaves in the blue sky, so warm.
The intone trees sing together with regard.
Notable green large larch trees and landform.
Smell of the restoring rain and wimple wood.
The red cedar revives and looks enlightens.
The sun was furtive and came out. We felt good.
Hearing an instrument tasteful and brightens.
Near pretty shrubs in the cherished glen
Seeing lovely flowers defines aesthete.
In a distance beautiful water then.
Romantic before the night sky entreat.
Adoring a high discrete mount aught.

Including beautiful besought retreat.
Admiring the painted horizon sky.
And being together with the sweet thought
Meadowsweet surrounding with my helpmeet.
Closing the window dreaming with a sigh.

10. Peaceful Beach Hymn

Waves whisper freedom and hearken a hymn.
Hear the billows and breeze of the beach.
Nocturnal sound quietly awaken them
Waves blend, transcend and capture shores reach
Picture the waves under the sunset
Always captures and calms the mood in the deep
Its' arranged colors cover the soul, yet
As you envision the lasting life keep;
Heaping sweet music as a fountain heard.
So soft of a sound through the years yearn.
Thank God for an impressive pleasing word;
Heeding the hymn of the healing beach learn.
God's word saves goes forth and never cease.
Acknowledge him, he is always there.
Be not afraid give the Lord a request.
And it shall not come back empty but peace.
And he will direct your path through prayer.
He's your confidence and has your steps blessed.

11. A Hymn of Prayer

I know as Jesus exists.

As the sun rises in the morning today.

The oceanic sound on the beach a bliss.

And the rainbow colors dance and convey.

And as the sunset blaze the fields.

Calm as the grassy mountain slopes with its stream.

The sweet odor of the meadow yields.

Existing as winning a trophy in a dream.

He provides me with provisions as the birds in a nest.

A happy reason to sing a song.

The bible tells us of his miracles to heal.

Knowing I have funds and health that I am blest.

He guides me in peace all my life long.

He was born, rose from the dead and saved us with zeal.

12. Love Letter in a Bottle

My love, I can't wait to see you.
I am writing you a letter today.
How you are? Please send me one too.
I am well, and I hope you are?
One day we will be together.
I long for your letter in a bottle.
And write you with a pen with a feather.
As earnest music to hear a glottal.
The moon whispers across the trees , leaves and stalk
As a flow of music across the waves
Interesting to meet my love and talk.
As the galliard with the sea behave
The waves ripples across the sand and mixes
As the rocks divide and form as a sand-cast.
Gallant ship displays as an anchor fixes.
In the wind my obsessed love is steadfast.
Soft sound of the waters entering the caves.
The pleasant look of the waters zest.
I dream of finding your letter that saves.
And sharing riches and a treasure chest.

I remember your same caress
We can run off to an island wish.
Its exciting to try to guess.
Walking on the beach seeing starfish.
Our love is as the deep waves in the water.
A quest to hear your many replies.
And as a ship's mast is tauter
That heads for the water's crest with sighs.
How long apart on the seas? I need your cheer.
The flowers bloom as the spring sired.
As a rose beautiful I wrote.
I will give you a diamond I need you near.
Just as the past you are admired.
Still love sick there is no antidote.

13. Open a Window and Write a Love Letter

Open a window to the radiant sunrise.
And fresh trees growing, giving fresh air likewise.
Then starting to write a love letter.
A rose brings forth a rose as a begetter.
Looking at the rose bushes dreaming obsessed.
With one day receiving roses impressed.
Thinking about the beauty of a rose.
As roses given and grow our love grows.
A full brilliant rose as lovely as a jewel.
A showpiece with beautiful accrual
Captivated by one another and the blooms.
Colorful the lovely garden illumes.
And remember walking on the shore.
Gorgeous view and taking a deep breath as before.
Then as the waves sparkle, flash and fizz.
Feeling warm splendid weather as it is.
Then charming and admiringly hug.
Pretty magical as music and snug.
With a perspective of peace immense.

And the profound sunset's presence.
And the starry skies alluring thence.
Proud to be overjoyed in marriage in the Spring.
And gleefully walk to the garden path and sing.
What intensely in love orchard's beauty bring.

14. A River Around a Mountain

I wonder about the mountain how high?
Notice the stars above the mount in the sky.
Enjoying its well form wishing to know.
That it holds the valley in its shadow
And as music the composer compiles.
And I like to see the river lap miles.
Arranged as the river runs in lovely form.
Sweeping and flowing downward just to perform
Sunrise and sets then the moon appears nearby
Who climbed the mountain across the river and why?
Orpheus with the lyre charms with poetry.
Eurydice his wife in past mythology.
Hebe carries water to fill its cup
Climbing and galloping the valleys up
As a marathoner running a race course
The energy of nature's peaceful force
Strong chasing circling amazing at a glance.
Around a mountain for miles performance
Harnessed and heaved-up downhill somewhere

To transform in the quarry there
River runs downward in a beautiful norm
Sweeps and flows as lovely music conform
Then it stopped sprinkling after an hour
Peaceful as a river after a shower.

15. Freedom and Goodwill

We come together with a popular pursuit,
Familiar faith and typical truths we dispute.
We come from a land to obtain, that has chosen us
For dreams, for privileges, for this reason thus --
Consider ourselves to have equal rights as those
Who would dare to care and take a chance to oppose
Those who venture out and do something different.
Do you know what is the purpose to what this meant?
They have freedom, they have rights, and they have a
voice.
They have humanity and a power of choice.
What do we say we have freedom of speech?
Freedom lives in the mind and soul of each.
The constitution can give a good opinion.
We possess a freedom in our dominion.
What is this faith that lies in men and women?
We remember the Liberty bell rang then.
Bought out of recession no more financial stress.
After struggling with depression brought to success.
As a searching safe sailor's beacon of light.

Shining through and bringing sight through the night.
As the Spirit of Freedom guarded and stop warfare.
And as God easily feeds the birds of the air.
The eagle flying before and after a storm.
The dove with the olive branch natural form.
Reassurance that God will let us see world peace.
nuclear warfare and its destruction cease.
Stop young men from dying as victims of war.
Protecting freedom, guarding goodwill therefore.
Protesting inhumane treatment is a freeman.
A kind heart and love for every human.
Love, live and last in nonviolence overall.

16. New Poetry Writer

A new writer went to share her knowledge of rhyme.
Wherefore she went to knock on a friend's door.
She went to sell her new book to pass the time.
Therefore a hand full of books she bore.
"I have a book of poems you would love", she said.
The friend said, "That's nice, let's talk, come on in".
And said, "I thought you were working, baking bread.
"No, I was just there buying bread again".
As the friend pushed back the heavy drapery
"This book of rhyme and rhythm can be yours"?
"I thought you were sewing pretty dresses to see.
"No, I stopped by the seamstress to sell literatures".
"I like something creative to read", said she.
"You will like poetry, its theme, style and form".
"And sonnets, odes and ballads you will agree".
"You're a house-sitter and not this writing brainstorm.
"No, I was in a house, they bought twelve, excuse me".
"They like the interesting book of rhyme, it's nice.
"It is fascinating the flow of words sound pretty."
"I know you are obsessed with my work, how I suffice".

"I'll buy six ", and she grabbed them with a jerk.
"Stay, read and have tea with cinnamon and spice."
Poetry is as flowers grow and blossom.
It needs sun shining to give it a perk.
And care as if it is in paradise.
Keep watering; it will grow big in its outcome.

17. The Old-Fashioned Girl

There was a schoolgirl in a town, not so small
Some students gathered in the hallway
As they hung around and some said to all,
With a laughing voice, "did you hear today"?
"The old-fashioned girl failed a class, OK."
Someone said, "are you sure? How do you know? "
"I thought she had a tutor to get an A".
Silly, she had no tutor, she was slow".
"She said, no to suicide and drugs, oh, no".
"Or she was bullied to commit suicide. "
"Then she met a Christian friend, not so-so".
"Someone to tutor her for free, if she tried".
"She met with her twice a week to confide".
"She changed her clothes well and her grades applied".

18. Knight and Damsel

The knight and damsel story you can guess.
On the ship's waves, wind, worry and woe.
How can the damsel be saved in distress?
From battling with the dragon's sorrow.
Sacred ship's precious load is a boggle.
As the force of waves roll, turn and flip,
Contrary, nonstop the ship will toggle.
Experience beauty as the waves dip.
Hark, large dragon, the damsel became faint.
The knight wrestled him, he was strong.
He fought the dragon forceful vigorous without restraint
He threw him back into the deep, he was wrong.
Thriving through the whirling whisking wave's bliss-out.
Damsel fine and clouds watery tinted within so bright.
Then washed out waxen waves throughout.
Adoring being in love with the waves light
When the brave feeling sunk in knowledge.
And count the years as stars shine and claves.
Behold the travelled past share slight dredge.
Feel curls clash clear turn all over to waves.

When lofty style soaked seen stayed by chance.
Which erstwhile storm a strong canopy sail?
Again times turned can make a new dance.
Summer's serenity slowly detail.
Like a lyre sound soft through the stars acquire.
Accept peace then of thyself do make.
Found from the place to perpetual admire.
Since knowing bristly will themselves forsake.
That thou among the severity must go.
Tell how brave to stop the vexing hence.
And fast as the brash show sadness grow.
Sure to become courageous thence.
Take the damsel to a happy land.
After fighting a dragon troublemaker.
It stopped terrorizing the ship and,
Then found his damsel safe like a matchmaker,
And put a wedding ring on her hand.
Adoring the sudden peacemaker.
They became a strong successful match
A latched catch to bring her to shore and sand
Spend time together as a merrymaker.
Get to know each other and be attached.

19. Dancing on a Ship

My sweet let us go away somewhere.
O yes, my love to a secluded shore.
As the sun softly sets with you near.
As the waves muffle and ruffle, therefore.
Hear the waves as a mellow music sound.
When will we escape in the water blue?
When, as the moon shines on the water around.
O my sweet, radiant as my love is new.
Caressing and watching the waves ripple.
Touching as the tender tides wrinkle.
It looks as art as if stirring stipple
Holding hands and see its light twinkle.
Then a delightful dinner that was well.
Then some extra energy and pep.
"My love why don't we dance, I am compelled".
Without delay with a stylish step.
Saying, "nice, your dancing is as a phenomenon;
As moon beams dance luxurious across the waves.
And as the waves look near the shore and on.
As the lovely sounds of the sea behaves".

In love dancing carefree through half the ship.
The bodies perform with rhythm and active.
Quick form on their feet, they continued to dance.
Romantic songs pleasing during courtship.
Like poetical beauty, creative and espressive.
Sounds fondly arranged themselves to entrance.

20. Under The Apple Tree

How your warm image came upon me.
Resting under the apple tree
Flowers bloom as our love; do you agree?
Before speaking, why do you sigh?
After rain danced on flowers you came by.
How beautiful the trees looked with the sky.
How happy to see your appearance near.
A nice day and the sky so clear.
The clouds floating and floral in cheer.
Pleasant to be together and not alone.
Your pretty content voice is so known.
Your satisfying smile is shown.
You filled me with the sweetness of your words.
We were as cheerful as two love birds
We kissed under the apple tree as birds heard.
We sat and watched two swan on a lake.
Their reflections with the moon until daybreak.
Our hearts melt in love as the moon reflection takes.

21. Stay Near to Jesus

Stay near to Jesus, he will help you.
Ask him anything you want.
He loves everybody; his love is true.
Don't worry he has the answer forefront.
He will help you every step of the way
Believe in prayer, trust and wait it succeeds.
Don't fear he will help you through the day.
Trust him and have faith with your needs.
Thank God, he cares and gives me a song.
About his kindness and goodness all day long